BEGINNING HISTORY

VICTORIAN
FACTORY WORKERS

D0709820

Dorothy Turner

Illustrated by Michael Bragg

Wayland

BEGINNING HISTORY

The Age of Exploration
The American West
Crusaders
Egyptian Farmers
Egyptian Pyramids
Family Life in World War II
Greek Cities
The Gunpowder Plot
Medieval Markets
Norman Castles

Plague and Fire
Roman Cities
Roman Soldiers
Saxon Villages
Tudor Sailors
Tudor Towns
Victorian Children
Victorian Factory Workers
Viking Explorers
Viking Warriors

All words that appear in **bold** are explained in the glossary on page 22.

Series Editor: Deborah Elliott
Book Editor: James Kerr
Designer: Helen White

First published in 1990 by Wayland (Publishers) Limited, 61 Western Road,
Hove, East Sussex BN3 1JD

© Copyright 1990 Wayland (Publishers) Limited

British Library Cataloguing in Publication Data
Turner, Dorothy *1944–*
Victorian factory workers.
1. Great Britain. Factories. Working conditions, history.
I. Title   II. Series
331.20941

HARDBACK ISBN 0-7502-0004-9

PAPERBACK ISBN 0-7502-0527-X

Typeset by Kalligraphics Limited, Horley, Surrey.
Printed in Italy by G. Canale & C.S.p.A., Turin.
Bound in Belgium by Casterman, S.A.

CONTENTS

FACTORIES AND MILLS

Until about 200 years ago, most British people lived in the countryside and worked on farms. Then great changes began. This was the time of the Industrial Revolution, when steam-powered machines were invented. These new machines could produce goods quickly and cheaply.

Factories were built, and filled with machines. Some factories, called mills, made cotton and wool cloth. Others produced lace, pottery or steel. But people were needed to work the machines. During the reign of Queen Victoria, many people left the countryside to work in factories. It was hard and tiring work.

THE WORKERS

Early Victorian factory workers were treated like **slaves** and forced to behave as if they were machines.

Above *Women labelling and packing pickles.*

Men, women and children worked as long as twelve hours a day for six days a week. **Overseers** watched them to make sure they did not break the rules or fall asleep. In some mills, workers were fined for whistling, or dropping a **bobbin**. Wages were low, especially for women and children. This was because factory owners wanted to make as much money as possible.

Above *Women and girls working in a mill.*

CHILDREN AT WORK

Above *A boy sweeping up in a cotton factory.*

Children who had no parents were often taken into factories to live and work. Some factory owners were cruel and gave them dirty rooms and scraps of food in return for long hours of labour. Children from poor families

Right *A cartoon from the 1840s showing children being beaten in a factory.*

also worked in factories. They had to earn money to help their parents.

Small children were given the job of crawling under dangerous machines to oil them or pick up threads. Many children fell asleep while working. Not surprisingly, many young workers died before they reached the age of sixteen.

HOW FACTORY WORKERS LIVED

Above *A painting of Sheffield from the 1850s.*

Streets of small, cheap houses were built around factories so that workers could live nearby. People walked to work early in the morning and walked back at night.

Right *These are the kinds of houses Victorian factory workers lived in.*

Most workers' houses had no running water or drains. Sometimes there was only one toilet for a whole street to share. Often, whole families lived in a single room. The houses were usually dark and damp. Many streets turned into **slums**. Factory workers who lived in slums suffered from bad health. They could not afford good food, warm clothes or medicines.

NEW CITIES

Eventually, small streets grew into big, smoky cities. This happened especially around the factories and coal-mines of the north of England and the Midlands.

In most cities, boys were given the job of climbing inside chimneys to clean out the **soot**. Many were burned, bruised or **suffocated** in the dark, narrow chimneys.

Life was hard for poor people in the cities. They could not afford doctors when they were ill, and there was no money for them if they were out of work. Many died young from disease.

FACTORY OWNERS

Factory owners ran their factories to make as much money as possible. This meant controlling workers with strict rules and punishments.

Many factory owners used cruel methods. Children were beaten with

TIME WASTER

straps by overseers. Adults were fined, or made to walk with cards or heavy stones round their necks, to show that they had done something wrong.

Factory owners generally lived in large, comfortable houses. Many of them made fortunes from the sale of goods produced in their factories.

Below *Many rich factory owners would have held tea parties like this.*

ROBERT OWEN

Not all factory owners were bad. Robert Owen was a mill owner who believed that all people deserved to be treated well.

At his mills in New Lanark, Scotland, he rewarded good workers.

Right *A picture of children being taught how to dance at Robert Owen's school.*

Below *A painting of New Lanark.*

He provided free schools for child workers and refused to employ children less than ten years old. The working day at his mills was shorter than at other factories, and meal breaks were longer. He built pleasant houses for his workers and set aside money to help them when they were in need.

GOING ON STRIKE

Factory workers' lives were hardest at the beginning of Queen Victoria's reign, during the 1830s and 1840s. Over the next 60 years, things slowly improved.

Parliament passed laws making it **illegal** for very young children to work in factories or for people to work for very long hours.

Workers also joined together in groups called **trade unions**. In the 1870s, **strikes** became legal. This gave unions the power to stop work until they got better conditions. Even so, life for factory workers was hard.

19

THE END OF AN ERA

By the end of Queen Victoria's reign, the working day was shorter. Electric lighting made factories brighter and safer. Some workers lived in new houses with running water. Many could afford to go on holiday to the seaside.

All men (but not women) could vote in **elections** and, in 1893, the **Labour Party** was formed. This gave workers their own voice in Parliament.

GLOSSARY

Bobbin A wooden reel around which wool or cotton thread is wound.

Elections When people vote for who should be in power.

Illegal Not allowed by law.

Labour Party A political party that tries to improve working and living conditions for ordinary working people.

Overseers People who made sure workers obeyed the rules and punished them if they did anything wrong.

Parliament The House of Commons and House of Lords. They meet to pass laws and decide how the country should be run.

Slaves People who are forced to work for no money.

Slums Dirty, overcrowded and unhealthy places where poor people are forced to live.

Soot The black powder left behind when coal is burned.

Strikes When workers refuse to work, usually because they want better pay and conditions.

Suffocated Unable to breathe.

Trade unions Groups of workers in a particular trade. Unions were set up to protect workers from being badly treated by managers and factory owners.

BOOKS TO READ

A Victorian Factory Worker by Stewart Ross (Wayland, 1985).

Dickens and the Victorians by Stewart Ross (Wayland, 1986).

Finding Out About Victorian Childhood by Pamela Harper (Batsford, 1986).

INDEX

Picture acknowledgements

The publishers would like to thank the following for providing the photographs in this book: C M Dixon 10 (bottom); E T Archives Limited 8 (top); The Mansell Collection 16 (bottom); Mary Evans Picture Library 6 (top), 8 (bottom); 15 (bottom), 16 (top); Syndication International 7 (top), 10 (top).